LANDMARKS IN MY COMMUNITY

TOWN HALL

BY SADIE SILVA

Please visit our website, www.garethstevens.com. For a free color catalog of all our high-quality books, call toll free 1-800-542-2595 or fax 1-877-542-2596.

Library of Congress Cataloging-in-Publication Data
Names: Silva, Sadie, author.
Title: Town hall / Sadie Silva.
Description: Buffalo, NY : Gareth Stevens, [2025] | Series: Landmarks in my community | Includes index. Identifiers: LCCN 2023034785 (print) | LCCN 2023034786 (ebook) | ISBN 9781538293225 (library binding) | ISBN 9781538293218 (paperback) | ISBN 9781538293232 (ebook)
Subjects: LCSH: Local government–Juvenile literature. | City halls–Juvenile literature. | Municipal officials and employees–Juvenile literature.
Classification: LCC JS78 .S58 2025 (print) | LCC JS78 (ebook) | DDC 320.8/5–dc23/eng/20230817
LC record available at https://lccn.loc.gov/2023034785
LC ebook record available at https://lccn.loc.gov/2023034786

Published in 2025 by
Gareth Stevens Publishing
2544 Clinton Street
Buffalo, NY 14224

Copyright © 2025 Gareth Stevens Publishing

Designer: Andrea Davison-Bartolotta
Editor: Caitie McAneney

Photo credits: Cover, p. 1 James R. Martin/Shutterstock.com; series art (page numbers) art_of_sun/Shutterstock.com; series art (map background) Marian Salabai/Shutterstock.com; p. 5 Waridsara_HappyChildren/Shutterstock.com; p. 7 Nolichuckyjake/Shutterstock.com; p. 9 refrina/Shutterstock.com; p. 11 Monkey Business Images/Shutterstock.com; p. 13 Sheila Fitzgerald/Shutterstock.com; p. 15 LightField Studios/Shutterstock.com; p. 17 Joni Hanebutt/Shutterstock.com; p. 19 vesperstock/Shutterstock.com; p. 21 WorldStockStudio/Shutterstock.com.

All rights reserved. No part of this book may be reproduced in any form without permission in writing from the publisher, except by a reviewer.

Printed in the United States of America

Some of the images in this book illustrate individuals who are models. The depictions do not imply actual situations or events.

CPSIA compliance information: Batch #CS25GS; For further information contact Gareth Stevens, New York, New York at 1-800-542-2595.

CONTENTS

Keeping It Local 4

Town Hall! 6

Town Hall Meetings 10

A Job at Town Hall 12

A Visit to Town Hall 14

A Gathering Place 16

Your Own Community 20

Glossary 22

For More Information 23

Index 24

Boldface words appear in the glossary.

Keeping It Local

Imagine you see a problem in your community or have an idea about how to make it better. You might want **recycling** bins at the local park or a new stop sign. Where can you go to talk to someone in **local government**?

Town Hall!

You can visit town hall! **Elected** leaders who make local laws work there. Different **departments** of local government may also have offices there. Towns and villages have town halls. Cities often have city halls.

Town hall is usually a building with many offices. Smaller towns may have smaller town halls with only a few rooms. Bigger towns and cities have larger town halls and city halls. They may have many floors and many offices.

Town Hall Meetings

Many town halls have a big room for town hall meetings. Anyone from the community can come to these meetings. People can speak their mind about what's important to them. People also visit town hall to pay bills and meet with local leaders.

A Job at Town Hall

Many people work at town hall. The mayor makes decisions about how a town or city works. City or town **council** members make local laws and **policies**. People in charge of certain departments, like **public works**, may also work there.

A Visit to Town Hall

Anyone can visit town hall! Some parts are open to the public, but some parts are not. You may need to make an appointment to talk to a local leader or worker. However, anyone can go to a town hall meeting.

A Gathering Place

Town halls are important places in any community. That's because they're places where people can gather. They can give ideas and get **information**. Community members can have their voices heard by people in power.

Town hall is often a place where people work on important community **projects**. People may also go there to vote for local leaders. This is just one more way in which people can have their voices heard in their local government.

Your Own Community

Have you ever gone to your town hall? Ask your parent or teacher where it is. You can ask who your local leaders are. You can write letters to local leaders or go to an open meeting. Make your voice heard!

GLOSSARY

council: A group of people meant to make decisions for a bigger group.

department: A part of a larger organization, such as a government.

elected: Voted into power.

information: Knowledge or facts that come from a source.

local government: The government for a town, village, or city.

policy: A plan of general and future decisions and positions.

project: A planned piece of work that has a specific goal.

public works: The government department that handles things, such as buildings and highways, that are for public use.

recycle: To treat something so it can be used again instead of thrown out.

FOR MORE INFORMATION

BOOKS

Boothroyd, Jennifer. *I Want to Be Mayor*. Minneapolis, MN: Bearport Publishing Company, 2024.

Stratton, Connor. *Local Governments*. Lake Elmo, MN: Focus Readers, 2024.

WEBSITES

Mayor
kids.britannica.com/kids/article/mayor/602777
Learn more about a mayor's job!

State and Local Governments
www.ducksters.com/history/us_state_and_local_governments.php
Explore fun facts about the different branches of local government.

Publisher's note to educators and parents: Our editors have carefully reviewed these websites to ensure that they are suitable for students. Many websites change frequently, however, and we cannot guarantee that a site's future contents will continue to meet our high standards of quality and educational value. Be advised that students should be closely supervised whenever they access the internet.

INDEX

cities, 6, 8, 12

council members, 12

laws, 6, 12

leaders, 6, 10, 14, 18, 20

local government, 4, 6, 18

mayor, 12

offices, 6, 8

park, 4

public works, 12

recycling, 4

town hall meetings, 10, 14, 20

villages, 6